Keep baby's head and toes warm and stylish with these adorable boots and hats sets. Created with the modern baby in mind, the colors are perfect for any occasion.

29

LEISURE ARTS, INC.
Maumelle, Arkansas

CASUAL BOOTS & HAT

SHOPPING LIST

Yarn (Medium Weight)

[4 ounces, 203 yards
(113 grams, 186 meters) per skein**]**:

- ☐ Taupe - 1 skein
- ☐ Green - 1 skein

Crochet Hooks

- ☐ Size F (3.75 mm) **and**
- ☐ Size H (5 mm)
  or sizes needed for gauge

Additional Supplies

- ☐ Split ring marker or scrap yarn
- ☐ 1" (25 mm) button - 3
- ☐ Sewing needle and thread

GAUGE INFORMATION

Hat

Gauge Swatch: 2" (5 cm) diameter

With larger size hook, work same as Rnds 1 and 2: 22 sc.

Boots

Gauge Swatch: 2" wide x 3{3½}" long/5 cm x 7.5{9} cm

With smaller size hook, work same as Sole: 32{36} sts.

STITCH GUIDE

SINGLE CROCHET 2 TOGETHER ***(abbreviated sc2tog)***

Pull up a loop in each of next 2 sts, YO and draw through all 3 loops on hook **(counts as one sc)**.

DOUBLE CROCHET 2 TOGETHER ***(abbreviated dc2tog)*** (uses next 2 sts)

★ YO, insert hook in next st, YO and pull up a loop, YO and draw through 2 loops on hook; repeat from ★ once **more**, YO and draw through all 3 loops on hook **(counts as one dc)**.

FRONT POST DOUBLE CROCHET ***(abbreviated FPdc)***

YO, insert hook from **front** to **back** around post of st indicated ***(Fig. A)***, YO and pull up a loop (3 loops on hook), (YO and draw through 2 loops on hook) twice.

BACK POST DOUBLE CROCHET ***(abbreviated BPdc)***

YO, insert hook from **back** to **front** around post of st indicated ***(Fig. B)***, YO and pull up a loop (3 loops on hook), (YO and draw through 2 loops on hook) twice.

Fig. A

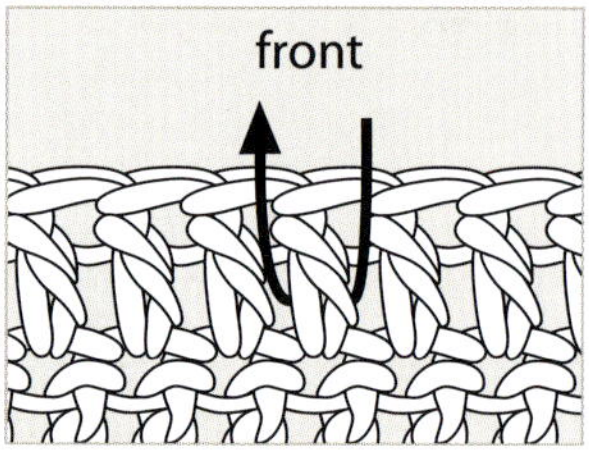

Fig. B

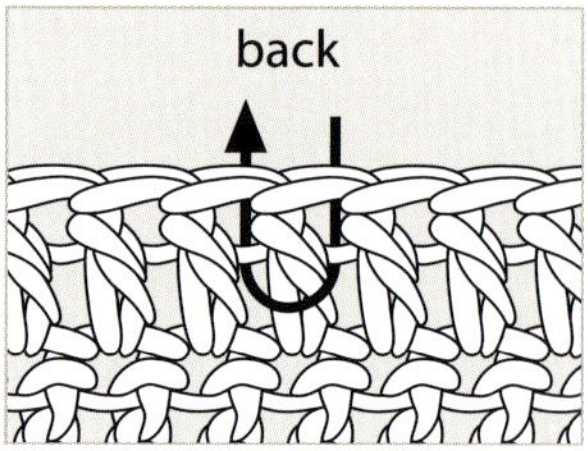

HAT

Finished Size: 14" (35.5 cm) circumference

Use larger size hook throughout.

Rnd 1 (Right side)**:** With Taupe, ch 4, 11 dc in fourth ch from hook; drop Taupe, with Green, join with slip st to first dc *(Fig. 4, page 46)*.

Note: Loop a short piece of yarn around any stitch to mark Rnd 1 as **right** side.

Rnd 2: Ch 1, 2 sc in same st as joining and in each dc around; drop Green, with Taupe, join with slip st to first sc: 22 sc.

Rnd 3: Ch 2 **(does not count as a st, now and throughout)**, dc in same st as joining, 2 dc in next sc, ★ dc in next sc, 2 dc in next sc; repeat from ★ around; drop Taupe, with Green, join with slip st to first dc: 33 dc.

Rnd 4: Ch 1, 2 sc in same st as joining, sc in next dc, 2 sc in next dc, ★ sc in next 2 dc, 2 sc in next dc; repeat from ★ around; drop Green, with Taupe, join with slip st to first sc: 45 sc.

Rnd 5: Ch 2, dc in same st as joining and in each sc around; drop Taupe, with Green, join with slip st to first dc.

Rnd 6: Ch 1, sc in same st as joining and in each dc around; drop Green, with Taupe, join with slip st to first sc.

Rnds 7-10: Repeat Rnd 5 and 6 twice; at end of Rnd 10, cut Green.

Rnd 11: Ch 2, dc in same st as joining and in each sc around; join with slip st to first dc.

Rnds 12-15: Ch 2, work FPdc around first st, work BPdc around each of next 2 sts, ★ work FPdc around next st, work BPdc around each of next 2 sts; repeat from ★ around; join with slip st to first FPdc.

Finish off.

Sew button to Hat.

BOOT (Make 2)
SIZE INFORMATION

Small: 2" wide x 3" long
(5 cm x 7.5 cm)
Medium: 2" wide x 3½" long
(5 cm x 9 cm)

Size Note: We have printed the instructions for the sizes in different colors to make it easier for you to find:
- Size Small in Blue
- Size Medium in Pink

Instructions in Black apply to both sizes.

Use smaller size hook throughout.

SOLE (Make one in Taupe and one in Green for **each** boot)

Ch 8{10}.

Rnd 1 (Right side)**:** Sc in second ch from hook and in each ch across to last ch, 4 hdc in last ch; working in free loops of beginning ch ***(Fig. 1, page 45)***, sc in next 5{7} chs, 3 sc in next ch; join with slip st to first sc: 18{22} sts.

Note: Loop a short piece of yarn around any stitch to mark Rnd 1 as **right** side.

Rnd 2: Ch 1, sc in same st as joining and in next 3{5} sc, hdc in next 2 sc, 2 dc in each of next 4 hdc, hdc in next 2 sc, sc in next 3{5} sc, 2 sc in each of last 3 sc; join with slip st to first sc: 25{29} sts.

Rnd 3: Ch 2 **(does not count as a st, now and throughout)**, hdc in same st as joining and in next 6{8} sts, 2 hdc in next dc, (hdc in next dc, 2 hdc in next dc) 3 times, hdc in next 5{7} sts, (sc in next sc, 2 sc in next sc) 3 times; join with slip st to first hdc, finish off: 32{36} sts.

On Green Sole, place split ring marker or scrap yarn in Front Loop Only of first hdc made on Rnd 3 for st placement *(Fig. 2, page 45)*.

Joining: Hold two Soles with **wrong** sides together, matching sts, and Green Sole facing you. Do **not** begin with slip knot on hook. Holding Taupe to the back and working through **both** loops of **both** pieces, insert hook in any st on Rnd 3, YO and pull up a loop, slip st in each st around; cut yarn. Remove hook from loop. Insert hook from **back** to **front** through center of first st, hook loop and draw through, YO and pull end through loop.

SIDES & TOE

Rnd 1 (Right side)**:** With Taupe Sole away from you and working in Back Loops Only, join Taupe with sc in marked loop *(see Joining With Sc, page 45)*; remove marker, sc in each st around; join with slip st to first sc: 32{36} sc.

Rnd 2: Ch 1, working in both loops, sc in same st as joining and in next 11{13} sc, dc2tog 8 times, sc in last 4{6} sc; join with slip st to first sc: 24{28} sts.

Rnd 3: Ch 1, sc in same st as joining and in next 11{13} sc, dc2tog 4 times, sc in last 4{6} sc; join with slip st to first sc: 20{24} sts.

Rnd 4: Ch 1, sc in same st as joining and in next 11{13} sc, sc2tog twice, sc in last 4{6} sc; join with slip st to first sc, do **not** finish off: 18{22} sc.

CUFF

Size Small Only - Rnd 1: Ch 2, dc in same st as joining and in each sc around; join with slip st to first dc.

Size Medium Only - Rnd 1: Ch 2, dc in same st as joining and in each sc around to last 2 sc, dc2tog; join with slip st to first dc: 21 dc.

Both Sizes - Rnds 2-6: Ch 2, work FPdc around first st, work BPdc around each of next 2 sts, ★ work FPdc around next st, work BPdc around each of next 2 sts; repeat from ★ around; join with slip st to first FPdc.

Finish off.

Sew a button to Cuff having a right and left boot.

CASUAL LOAFERS & HAT

SHOPPING LIST

Yarn (Medium Weight)

[3.5 ounces, 170 yards (100 grams, 156 meters) per skein]:

- ☐ Tan - 1 skein
- ☐ Blue - 1 skein

Crochet Hooks

- ☐ Size F (3.75 mm) **and**
- ☐ Size H (5 mm)

or sizes needed for gauge

Additional Supplies

- ☐ Split ring marker or scrap yarn
- ☐ Yarn needle
- ☐ Sewing needle and thread (for Hat only)
- ☐ 1" (25 mm) button (for Hat only)

GAUGE INFORMATION

Hat

Gauge Swatch: 2½" (6.25 cm) diameter

With larger size hook, work same as Rnds 1-3: 21 hdc.

Loafers

Gauge Swatch: 2" wide x 3{3½}" long/5 cm x 7.5{9} cm

With smaller size hook, work same as Sole: 32{36} sts.

STITCH GUIDE

SINGLE CROCHET 2 TOGETHER ***(abbreviated sc2tog)***

Pull up a loop in each of next 2 sts, YO and draw through all 3 loops on hook **(counts as one sc)**.

HAT

Finished Size: 14" (35.5 cm) circumference

Use larger size hook throughout.

Rnd 1 (Right side)**:** With Tan, ch 2; 7 hdc in second ch from hook; do **not** join, place marker to indicate beginning of rnd ***(see Markers, page 44)***.

Note: Loop a short piece of yarn around any stitch to mark Rnd 1 as **right** side.

Rnd 2: 2 Hdc in each hdc around: 14 hdc.

Rnd 3: (Hdc in next hdc, 2 hdc in next hdc) around: 21 hdc.

Rnd 4: (Hdc in next 2 hdc, 2 hdc in next hdc) around: 28 hdc.

Rnd 5: (Hdc in next 3 hdc, 2 hdc in next hdc) around: 35 hdc.

Rnd 6: (Hdc in next 4 hdc, 2 hdc in next hdc) around: 42 hdc.

Rnds 7-11: Hdc in each hdc around.

Slip st in next hdc; finish off.

Rnd 12: With **right** side facing, join Blue with slip st in same st as slip st; ch 1, hdc in same st and in each hdc around; join with slip st to first hdc.

Rnds 13-15: Ch 1, hdc in same st as joining and in each hdc around; join with slip st to first hdc.

Finish off.

TAB

With Tan, ch 6.

Row 1 (Right side)**:** Sc in second ch from hook and in each ch across: 5 sc.

Note: Mark Row 1 as **right** side.

Rows 2-13: Ch 1, turn; sc in each sc across.

Row 14: Turn; beginning in first sc, sc2tog, sc in next sc, sc2tog: 3 sc.

Row 15: Turn; beginning in first sc, sc2tog, beginning in same st, sc2tog, finish off leaving a long end for sewing.

Using photo as a guide for placement:
With double strand of Tan, weave through sts on Rnd 12.
With double strand of Blue, weave through sts around Tab.
Placing beginning ch of Tab to inside of hat and last row on the outside, sew in place.
Sew button to Tab.

LOAFER (Make 2)

SIZE INFORMATION

Small: 2" wide x 3" long (5 cm x 7.5 cm)

Medium: 2" wide x 3½" long (5 cm x 9 cm)

Size Note: We have printed the instructions for the sizes in different colors to make it easier for you to find:

- Size Small in Blue
- Size Medium in Pink

Instructions in Black apply to both sizes.

Use smaller size hook throughout.

SOLE (Make one in Tan and one in Blue for **each** loafer)

Ch 8{10}.

Rnd 1 (Right side)**:** Sc in second ch from hook and in each ch across to last ch, 4 hdc in last ch; working in free loops of beginning ch ***(Fig. 1, page 45)***, sc in next 5{7} chs, 3 sc in next ch; join with slip st to first sc: 18{22} sts.

Note: Loop a short piece of yarn around any stitch to mark Rnd 1 as **right** side.

Rnd 2: Ch 1, sc in same st as joining and in next 3{5} sc, hdc in next 2 sc, 2 dc in each of next 4 hdc, hdc in next 2 sc, sc in next 3{5} sc, 2 sc in each of last 3 sc; join with slip st to first sc: 25{29} sts.

Rnd 3: Ch 2 (**does not count as a st**), hdc in same st as joining and in next 6{8} sts, 2 hdc in next dc, (hdc in next dc, 2 hdc in next dc) 3 times, hdc in next 5{7} sts, (sc in next sc, 2 sc in next sc) 3 times; join with slip st to first hdc, finish off: 32{36} sts.

On Tan Sole, place split ring marker or scrap yarn in Front Loop Only of first hdc made on Rnd 3 for st placement ***(Fig. 2, page 45)***.

Joining: Hold two Soles with **wrong** sides together, matching sts, and Blue Sole facing you. Do **not** begin with slip knot on hook. Holding Tan to the back and working through **both** loops of **both** pieces, insert hook in any st on Rnd 3, YO and pull up a loop, slip st in each st around; cut yarn. Remove hook from loop. Insert hook from **back** to **front** through center of first st, hook loop and draw through, YO and pull end through loop.

SIDES & TOE

Rnd 1 (Right side)**:** With Tan Sole away from you and working in Back Loops Only, join Tan with sc in marked loop (***see Joining With Sc, page 45)***; remove marker, sc in each st around; join with slip st to first sc: 32{36} sc.

Rnd 2: Ch 1, sc in both loops of each sc around; join with slip st to first sc.

Rnd 3: Ch 1, sc in same st as joining and in next 11{13} sc, working in Back Loops Only, sc2tog 8 times, sc in **both** loops of last 4{6} sc; join with slip st to first sc: 24{28} sc.

Rnd 4: Ch 1, sc in same st as joining and in next 11{13} sc, sc2tog 4 times, sc in last 4{6} sc; join with slip st to first sc: 20{24} sc.

Rnd 5: Ch 1, sc in same st as joining and in next 11{13} sc, sc2tog twice, sc in last 4{6} sc; join with slip st to first sc: 18{22} sc.

Rnd 6: Ch 1, sc in same st as joining and in next 12{14} sc, (slip st, ch 2, dc) in next sc, (dc, ch 2, slip st) in next sc, sc in last 3{5} sc; join with slip st to first sc; finish off.

Using photo as a guide for placement and a 12" (30.5 cm) length of Blue, weave through sts on last rnd.

HEEL TAB

With Blue, ch 4.

Row 1: Sc in second ch from hook and in each ch across: 3 sc.

Rows 2-10: Ch 1, turn; sc in each sc across.

Row 11: Turn; beginning in first sc, sc2tog, beginning in same st, sc2tog: 2 sc.

Row 12: Turn; beginning in first sc, sc2tog; finish off leaving a long end for sewing.

Placing beginning ch of Heel Tab to inside of loafer and last row on the outside, sew in place.

HIGH-TOP MOCCASINS & HAT

EASY

SHOPPING LIST

Yarn (Medium Weight) MEDIUM 4

[4 ounces, 203 yards
(113 grams, 186 meters) per skein]:

- ☐ Grey - 1 skein
- ☐ Green - 1 skein
- ☐ Blue - 1 skein
- ☐ Gold - 1 skein

Crochet Hooks

- ☐ Size F (3.75 mm) **and**
- ☐ Size H (5 mm)
  or sizes needed for gauge

Additional Supplies

- ☐ Split ring marker or scrap yarn
- ☐ Yarn needle

GAUGE INFORMATION

Hat

Gauge Swatch: 3" (7.5 cm) square

With larger size hook and Grey, ch 11.

Row 1: Sc in second ch from hook and in each ch across: 10 sc.

Rows 2-12: Ch 1, turn; sc in each sc across.

Finish off.

Moccasins

Gauge Swatch: 2" wide x 3{3½}" long/5 cm x 7.5{9} cm

With smaller size hook, work same as Sole: 32{36} sts.

STITCH GUIDE

SPLIT SINGLE CROCHET ***(abbreviated Split sc)***

Insert hook between legs of next st ***(Fig. A)***, YO and pull up a loop, YO and draw through both loops on hook.

Fig. A

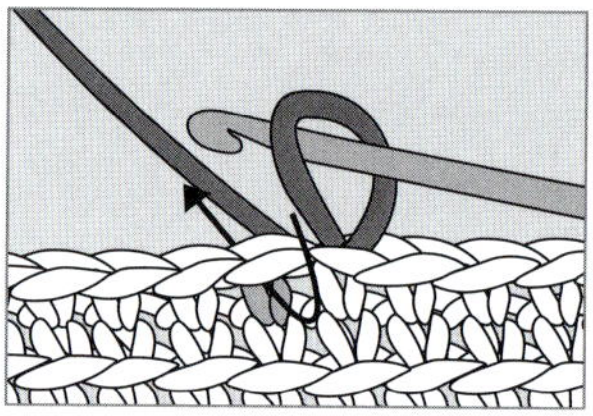

SINGLE CROCHET 2 TOGETHER ***(abbreviated sc2tog)***

Pull up a loop in each of next 2 sts, YO and draw through all 3 loops on hook **(counts as one sc)**.

DOUBLE CROCHET 2 TOGETHER ***(abbreviated dc2tog)*** (uses next 2 sts)

★ YO, insert hook in next st, YO and pull up a loop, YO and draw through 2 loops on hook; repeat from ★ once **more**, YO and draw through all 3 loops on hook **(counts as one dc)**.

HAT

Finished Size: 14" (35.5 cm) circumference

Use larger size hook throughout.

With Grey and leaving a long end for sewing, ch 46.

Rnd 1 (Right side)**:** Sc in second ch from hook and in each ch across; join with slip st to first sc: 45 sc.

Note: Loop a short piece of yarn around any stitch to mark Rnd 1 as **right** side.

Rnd 2: Ch 1, work Split sc in each sc around; join with slip st to first Split sc.

Rnds 3 and 4: Ch 1, work Split sc in each Split sc around; join with slip st to first Split sc.

Rnd 5: Ch 1, sc in Back Loop Only ***(Fig. 1, page 45)*** of each st around; do **not** join, place marker to indicate beginning of rnd ***(see Markers, page 44)***.

Rnds 6-17: Sc in each sc around.

Rnd 18: (Sc2tog, sc in next 3 sc) around: 36 sc.

Rnd 19: (Sc2tog, sc in next 2 sc) around: 27 sc.

Rnd 20: (Sc2tog, sc in next sc) around: 18 sc.

Rnd 21: Sc2tog around: 9 sc.

Rnd 22: Sc in each sc around; slip st in next sc, finish off leaving a long end for sewing.

Thread yarn needle with long end and weave needle through sts on Rnd 22 ***(Fig. 5, page 46)***, gather tightly and secure end.

Thread yarn needle with beginning end and sew through chs at base of first and last sc; secure end.

DUPLICATE SPLIT SC

Duplicate Split sc is worked over the first Split sc rnd (Rnd 2). Each stitch forms a V and you want to completely cover that V so that the design appears to have been worked into the fabric. Thread a yarn needle with an 18" (45.5 cm) length of Blue.

With **right** side facing and beginning at first stitch on Rnd 2, bring the needle up from the **wrong** side between the strands of yarn on Rnd 2 at the base of the V, leaving an end to be woven in later ***(Fig. B)***. Follow the right side of the V up and insert the needle from **right** to **left** under the strands of the V immediately above, keeping the yarn on top of the stitch ***(Fig. C)***, and draw through. Insert the needle back through the bottom of the same stitch where the first stitch began ***(duplicate Split sc completed)***. Work over every other stitch around, matching tension of fabric to avoid puckering.

Fig. B

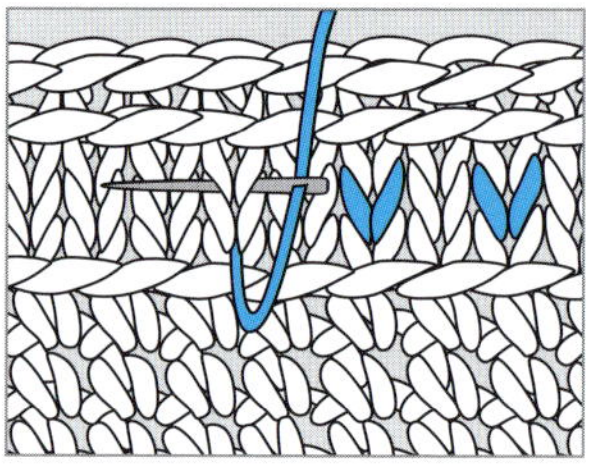

Fig. C

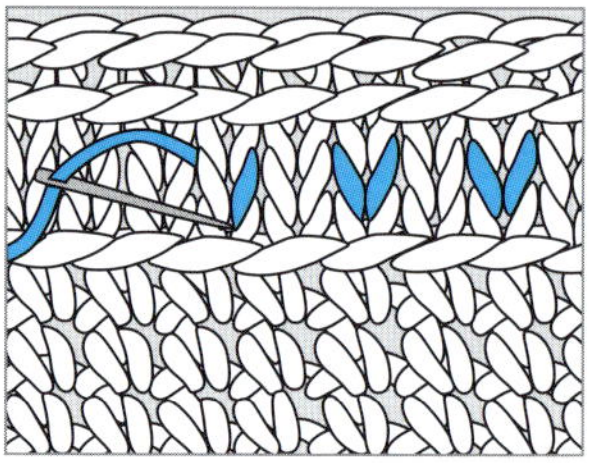

With Gold, work duplicate Split sc over each unworked stitch of Rnd 2.

Repeat duplicate Split sc on Rnd 3 alternating colors.

With double strand of Green, weave through sts on Rnd 1; secure ends to **wrong** side.

With double strand of Green, weave through sts on Rnd 4. Secure ends of one strand on **wrong** side; with remaining strand, tie ends in a bow.

MOCCASIN (Make 2)
SIZE INFORMATION

Small: 2" wide x 3" long
(5 cm x 7.5 cm)
Medium: 2" wide x 3½" long
(5 cm x 9 cm)

Size Note: We have printed the instructions for the sizes in different colors to make it easier for you to find:
· Size Small in Blue
· Size Medium in Pink
Instructions in Black apply to both sizes.

Use smaller size hook throughout.

SOLE (Make one in Grey and one in Green for **each** moccasin)

Ch 8{10}.

Rnd 1 (Right side)**:** Sc in second ch from hook and in each ch across to last ch, 4 hdc in last ch; working in free loops of beginning ch ***(Fig. 1, page 45)***, sc in next 5{7} chs, 3 sc in next ch; join with slip st to first sc: 18{22} sts.

Note: Loop a short piece of yarn around any stitch to mark Rnd 1 as **right** side.

Rnd 2: Ch 1, sc in same st as joining and in next 3{5} sc, hdc in next 2 sc, 2 dc in each of next 4 hdc, hdc in next 2 sc, sc in next 3{5} sc, 2 sc in each of last 3 sc; join with slip st to first sc: 25{29} sts.

Rnd 3: Ch 2 **(does not count as a st)**, hdc in same st as joining and in next 6{8} sts, 2 hdc in next dc, (hdc in next dc, 2 hdc in next dc) 3 times, hdc in next 5{7} sts, (sc in next sc, 2 sc in next sc) 3 times; join with slip st to first hdc, finish off: 32{36} sts.

On Grey Sole, place split ring marker or scrap yarn in Front Loop Only of first hdc made on Rnd 3 for st placement ***(Fig. 2, page 45)***.

Joining: Hold two Soles with **wrong** sides together, matching sts, and Green Sole facing you. Do **not** begin with slip knot on hook. Holding Grey to the back and working through **both** loops of **both** pieces, insert hook in any st on Rnd 3, YO and pull up a loop, slip st in each st around; cut yarn. Remove hook from loop. Insert hook from **back** to **front** through center of first st, hook loop and draw through, YO and pull end through loop.

SIDES & TOE

Rnd 1 (Right side)**:** With Grey Sole away from you and working in Back Loops Only, join Grey with sc in marked loop ***(see Joining With Sc, page 45)***; remove marker, sc in each st around; join with slip st to first sc: 32{36} sc.

Rnd 2: Ch 1, sc in both loops of each sc around; join with slip st to first sc.

Rnd 3: Ch 1, sc in same st as joining and in next 11{13} sc, working in Back Loops Only, dc2tog 8 times, sc in **both** loops of last 4{6} sc; join with slip st to first sc: 24{28} sts.

Rnd 4: Ch 1, sc in same st as joining and in next 11{13} sc, dc2tog 4 times, sc in last 4{6} sc; join with slip st to first sc: 20{24} sts.

Rnd 5: Ch 1, sc in same st as joining and in next 11{13} sc, dc2tog twice, sc in last 4{6} sc; join with slip st to first sc: 18{22} sc.

Rnds 6-11: Ch 1, sc in each sc around; join with slip st to first sc.

Rnd 12: Ch 1, sc in Back Loop Only of each sc around; join with slip st to first sc.

Rnd 13: Ch 1, work Split sc in each sc around; join with slip st to first Split sc.

Rnd 14: Ch 1, work Split sc in each Split sc around; join with slip st to first Split sc.

Rnd 15: Ch 1, sc in Back Loop Only of each st around; join with slip st to first sc, finish off.

With Blue, work duplicate Split sc over every other stitch on Rnd 13, matching tension of fabric to avoid puckering.

With Gold, work duplicate Split sc over each unworked stitch on Rnd 13.

FRINGE

Cut a piece of cardboard 2" (5 cm) square. Wind Grey loosely and evenly around the cardboard until the card is filled, then cut across one end; repeat as needed. Fold one strand of yarn in half. Insert hook from top to bottom in free loop of first stitch on Rnd 11 (unused loop after working in back loops). Draw the folded end up through the stitch and pull the loose ends through the folded end (***Fig. D***); draw the knot up tightly ***(Fig. E)***. Repeat in each stitch around. Trim the ends.

Fig. D

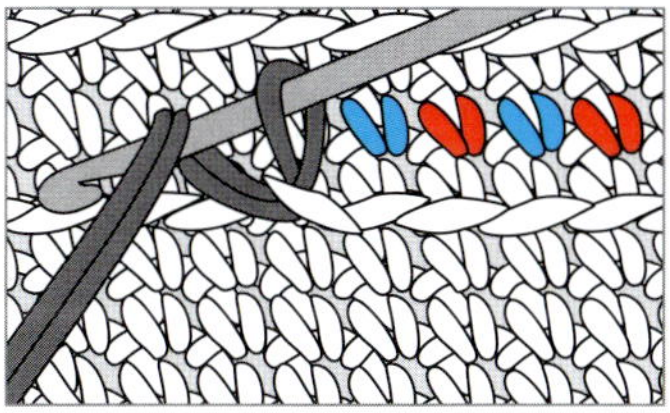

Fig. E

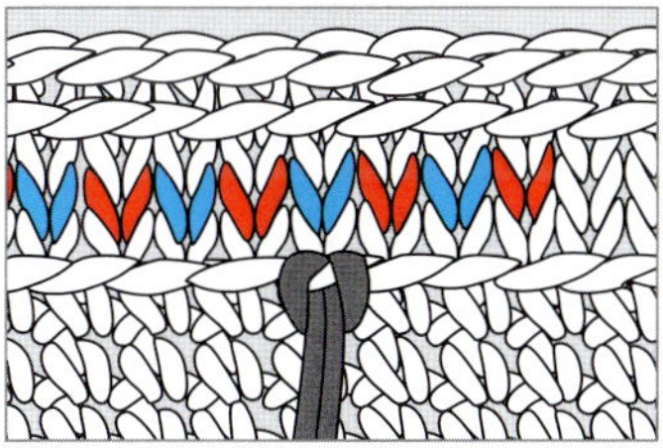

TRIM

Using photo as a guide for placement and beginning at opposite sides of boots for right and left boot, weave a single strand of Green through stitches on last rnd; tie ends in a bow.

LACY CUFF BOOTS & HAT

SHOPPING LIST

Yarn (Medium Weight) MEDIUM 4

[3.5 ounces, 170 yards (100 grams, 156 meters) per skein]:

- ☐ Rose - 1 skein
- ☐ Grey - 1 skein
- ☐ White - 1 skein

Crochet Hooks

- ☐ Size F (3.75 mm) **and**
- ☐ Size H (5 mm)

or sizes needed for gauge

Additional Supplies

- ☐ Split ring marker or scrap yarn
- ☐ Yarn needle

GAUGE INFORMATION

Hat

Gauge Swatch:
2" (5 cm) diameter

With larger size hook, work same as Rnds 1 and 2: 20 sc.

Boots

Gauge Swatch: 2" wide x 3{3½}" long/5 cm x 7.5{9} cm

With smaller size hook, work same as Sole: 32{36} sts.

STITCH GUIDE

TREBLE CROCHET
(abbreviated tr)

YO twice, insert hook in st indicated, YO and pull up a loop (4 loops on hook), (YO and draw through 2 loops on hook) 3 times.

SINGLE CROCHET 2 TOGETHER
(abbreviated sc2tog)

Pull up a loop in each of next 2 sts, YO and draw through all 3 loops on hook **(counts as one sc)**.

DOUBLE CROCHET 2 TOGETHER
(abbreviated dc2tog)
(uses next 2 sts)

★ YO, insert hook in next st, YO and pull up a loop, YO and draw through 2 loops on hook; repeat from ★ once **more**, YO and draw through all 3 loops on hook **(counts as one dc)**.

HAT

Finished Size: 14" (35.5 cm) circumference

Use larger size hook throughout.

Rnd 1 (Right side)**:** With Rose, ch 4; 10 dc in fourth ch from hook; join with slip st to first dc: 10 dc.

Note: Loop a short piece of yarn around any stitch to mark Rnd 1 as **right** side.

Rnd 2: Ch 1, 2 sc in same st as joining and in each dc around: 20 sc.

Rnd 3: Ch 3 **(counts as first dc, now and throughout)**, 2 dc in next sc, (dc in next sc, 2 dc in next sc) around; join with slip st to first dc: 30 dc.

Rnd 4: Ch 1, 2 sc in same st as joining, sc in next dc, 2 sc in each of next 2 dc, sc in next dc, 2 sc in next dc, (sc in next 2 dc, 2 sc in next dc) around; join with slip st to first sc: 42 sc.

Rnd 5: Ch 4 (**counts as first tr**), **turn**; skip next 4 sc, tr in next sc, ch 1, working in **front** of tr just made ***(Fig. 3a, page 46)***, tr in third skipped sc, ★ skip next 2 sc, tr in next sc, ch 1, working in **front** of tr just made, tr in first skipped sc; repeat from ★ around, working **behind** first tr ***(Fig. 3b, page 46)***, tr in second skipped sc, ch 1; join with slip st to first tr: 28 tr and 14 ch-1 sps.

Rnd 6: Ch 1, turn; sc in same st as joining and in each ch-1 sp and each tr around; join with slip st to first sc: 42 sc.

Rnds 7-9: Repeat Rnds 5 and 6 once, then repeat Rnd 5 once **more**: 28 tr and 14 ch-1 sps.

Rnd 10: Ch 1, turn; sc in same st as joining and in each ch-1 sp and each tr around; drop Rose, with Grey, join with slip st to first sc ***(Fig. 4, page 46)***: 42 sc.

Rnd 11: Ch 1, sc in same st as joining and in each sc around; drop Grey, with Rose, join with slip st to first sc.

Rnd 12: Ch 1, turn; sc in same st as joining and in each sc around; drop Rose, with Grey, join with slip st to first sc.

Rnd 13: Ch 1, sc in same st as joining and in each sc around; cut Grey, with Rose, join with slip st to first sc.

Rnd 14: Ch 3, skip next sc, ★ slip st in next sc, ch 3, skip next sc; repeat from ★ around; join with slip st to first slip st, finish off.

FLOWER

With Rose, ch 4; join with slip st to form a ring.

Rnd 1 (Right side)**:** 6 Sc in ring; join with slip st to first sc, finish off leaving a long end for sewing.

Note: Mark Rnd 1 as **right** side.

Rnd 2: With **right** side facing; join White with slip st in first sc, ch 2, (dc, ch 1, slip st) in same st, (slip st, ch 2, dc, ch 1, slip st) in each sc around; join with slip st to joining slip st, finish off.

Using photo as a guide for placement, sew Flower to Hat.

BOOT (Make 2)
SIZE INFORMATION

Small: 2" wide x 3" long
(5 cm x 7.5 cm)
Medium: 2" wide x 3½" long
(5 cm x 9 cm)

Size Note: We have printed the instructions for the sizes in different colors to make it easier for you to find:
· Size Small in Blue
· Size Medium in Pink
Instructions in Black apply to both sizes.

Use smaller size hook throughout.

SOLE (Make 2 for **each** boot)

With Grey, ch 8{10}.

Rnd 1 (Right side)**:** Sc in second ch from hook and in each ch across to last ch, 4 hdc in last ch; working in free loops of beginning ch ***(Fig. 1, page 45)***, sc in next 5{7} chs, 3 sc in next ch; join with slip st to first sc: 18{22} sts.

Note: Loop a short piece of yarn around any stitch to mark Rnd 1 as **right** side.

Rnd 2: Ch 1, sc in same st as joining and in next 3{5} sc, hdc in next 2 sc, 2 dc in each of next 4 hdc, hdc in next 2 sc, sc in next 3{5} sc, 2 sc in each of last 3 sc; join with slip st to first sc: 25{29} sts.

Rnd 3: Ch 2 **(does not count as a st)**, hdc in same st as joining and in next 6{8} sts, 2 hdc in next dc, (hdc in next dc, 2 hdc in next dc) 3 times, hdc in next 5{7} sts, (sc in next sc, 2 sc in next sc) 3 times; join with slip st to first hdc, finish off: 32{36} sts.

On one Sole for each boot, place split ring marker or scrap yarn in Front Loop Only of first hdc made on Rnd 3 for st placement ***(Fig. 2, page 45)***.

Joining: Hold two Soles with **wrong** sides together, matching sts, and marked Sole on bottom. Do **not** begin with slip knot on hook. Holding Rose to the back and working through **both** loops of **both** pieces, insert hook in any st on Rnd 3, YO and pull up a loop, slip st in each st around; cut yarn. Remove hook from loop. Insert hook from **back** to **front** through center of first st, hook loop and draw through, YO and pull end through loop.

SIDES & TOE

Rnd 1 (Right side)**:** With marked Sole away from you and working in Back Loops Only; join Grey with sc in marked loop ***(see Joining With Sc, page 45)***; remove marker, sc in each st around; drop Grey, with Rose; join with slip st to first sc ***(Fig. 4, page 46)***: 32{36} sc.

Rnd 2: Ch 1, sc in both loops of each sc around; drop Rose, with Grey; join with slip st to first sc.

Rnd 3: Ch 1, sc in same st as joining and in next 11{13} sc, dc2tog 8 times, sc in next 4{6} sc; drop Grey, with Rose; join with slip st to first sc: 24{28} sts.

Rnd 4: Ch 1, sc in same st as joining and in next 11{13} sc, dc2tog 4 times, sc in next 4{6} sc; drop Rose, with Grey; join with slip st to first sc: 20{24} sts.

Rnd 5: Ch 1, sc in same st as joining and in next 11{13} sc, dc2tog twice, sc in last 4{6} sc; drop Grey, with Rose; join with slip st to first sc: 18{22} sc.

Rnd 6: Ch 1, sc in same st as joining and in next 11{13} sc, sc2tog, sc in last 4{6} sc; cut Rose, with Grey; join with slip st to first sc: 17{21} sc.

Rnd 7: Ch 1, sc in each sc around; do not join, place marker to indicate beginning of rnd ***(see Markers, page 44)***.

Rnds 8-13: Sc in each sc around.

Slip st in next sc, finish off.

LACY CUFF

Size Small Only - Rnd 1: With **wrong** side facing and working in Back Loops Only; join Rose with sc in same st as slip st; (sc in next 3 sc, 2 sc in next sc) around; join with slip st to first sc: 21 sc.

Size Medium Only - Rnd 1: With **wrong** side facing and working in Back Loops Only; join Rose with sc in same st as slip st; sc in next 5 sc, 2 sc in next sc, (sc in next 6 sc, 2 sc in next sc) twice; join with slip st to first sc: 24 sc.

Both Sizes - Rnd 2: Ch 4 **(counts as first tr)**, **turn**; skip next 4 sc, tr in next sc, ch 1, working in **front** of tr just made ***(Fig. 3a, page 46)***, tr in third skipped sc, ★ skip next 2 sc, tr in next sc, ch 1, working in **front** of tr just made, tr in first skipped sc; repeat from ★ around, working **behind** first tr ***(Fig. 3b, page 46)***, tr in second skipped sc, ch 1; join with slip st to first tr: 14{16} tr and 7{8} ch-1 sps.

Rnd 3: Ch 1, turn; sc in same st as joining and in each ch-1 sp and each tr around; join with slip st to first sc: 21{24} sc.

Rnd 4: Repeat Rnd 2.

Rnd 5: Ch 3, turn; slip st in same st as joining, (slip st, ch 3, slip st) in each ch-1 sp and in each tr around; finish off.

Fold Cuff down.

FLOWER

Work same as Flower on Hat. Using photo as a guide for placement, sew a Flower to each Cuff having a right and left boot.

HIGH-TOP SNEAKERS & HAT

EASY

SHOPPING LIST

Yarn (Medium Weight) MEDIUM 4

[5 ounces, 256 yards
(141 grams, 134 meters) per skein]:

- ☐ White - 1 skein
- ☐ Orange - 1 skein

[4 ounces, 212 yards
(113 grams, 194 meters) per skein]:

- ☐ Grey - 1 skein

Crochet Hooks

- ☐ Size F (3.75 mm) **and**
- ☐ Size H (5 mm)
  or sizes needed for gauge

Additional Supplies

- ☐ Split ring marker or scrap yarn
- ☐ Yarn needle

GAUGE INFORMATION

Hat

Gauge Swatch: 2¼" (5.75 cm) diameter
With larger size hook, work same as Rnds 1 and 2: 22 dc.

Sneakers

Gauge Swatch: 2" wide x 3{3½}" long/5 cm x 7.5{9} cm
With smaller size hook, work same as Sole: 32{36} sts.

STITCH GUIDE

SINGLE CROCHET 2 TOGETHER ***(abbreviated sc2tog)***

Pull up a loop in each of next 2 sts, YO and draw through all 3 loops on hook **(counts as one sc)**.

DOUBLE CROCHET 2 TOGETHER ***(abbreviated dc2tog)*** (uses next 2 sts)

★ YO, insert hook in next st, YO and pull up a loop, YO and draw through 2 loops on hook; repeat from ★ once **more**, YO and draw through all 3 loops on hook **(counts as one dc)**.

HAT

Finished Size: 14" (35.5 cm) circumference

Use larger size hook throughout.

Rnd 1 (Right side)**:** With White, ch 4; 11 dc in fourth ch from hook; join with slip st to first dc: 11 dc.

Note: Loop a short piece of yarn around any stitch to mark Rnd 1 as **right** side.

Rnd 2: Ch 2 **(does not count as a st, now and throughout)**, 2 dc in same st as joining and in each dc around; join with slip st to first dc: 22 dc.

Rnd 3: Ch 2, dc in same st as joining, 2 dc in next dc, (dc in next dc, 2 dc in next dc) around; join with slip st to first dc: 33 dc.

Rnd 4: Ch 2, dc in same st as joining and in next dc, 2 dc in next dc, (dc in next 2 dc, 2 dc in next dc) around; join with slip st to first dc: 44 dc.

Rnds 5 and 6: Ch 2, dc in same st as joining and in each dc around; join with slip st to first dc.

Finish off.

Rnd 7: With **right** side facing, join Orange with sc in same st as joining ***(see Joining with Sc, page 45)***; ch 1, skip next dc, ★ sc in next dc, ch 1, skip next dc; repeat ★ around; join with slip st to first sc, finish off: 22 sc and 22 ch-1 sps.

Rnd 8: With **right** side facing, join Grey with sc in first ch-1 sp; ch 1, (sc in next ch-1 sp, ch 1) around; join with slip st to first sc, finish off.

Rnd 9: With **right** side facing, join Orange with sc in first ch-1 sp; ch 1, (sc in next ch-1 sp, ch 1) around; join with slip st to first sc, finish off.

Rnds 10 and 11: Repeat Rnds 8 and 9.

Rnd 12: With **right** side facing, join White with dc in any sc ***(see Joining with Dc, page 45)***; dc in each ch-1 sp and in each sc around; join with slip st to first dc: 44 dc.

Rnd 13: Ch 2, dc in same st as joining and in each dc around; join with slip st to first dc, finish off.

Rnd 14: With **right** side facing, join Orange with slip st in any dc; ch 1, working from **left** to **right**, ★ insert hook in st to right of hook ***(Fig. A)***, YO and draw through, under and to left of loop on hook (2 loops on hook) ***(Fig. B)***, YO and draw through both loops on hook ***(Fig. C)*** **(reverse sc made, *Fig. D*)**; repeat from ★ around; join with slip st to first st, finish off.

Fig. A

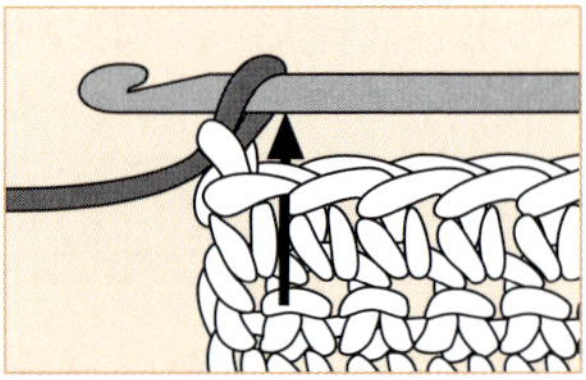

Fig. B

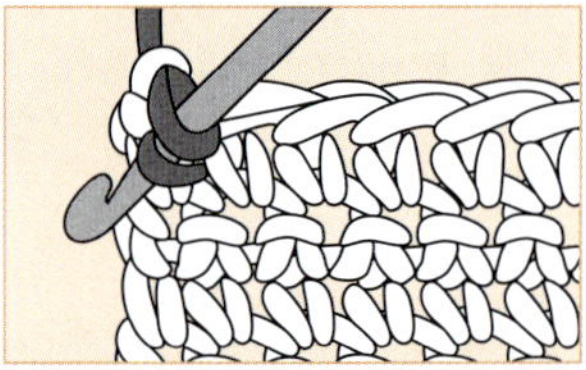

Fig. C

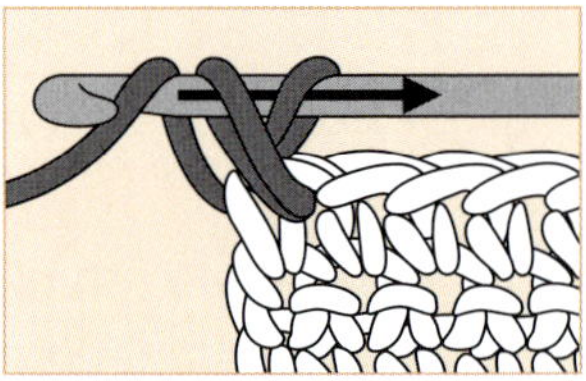

Fig. D

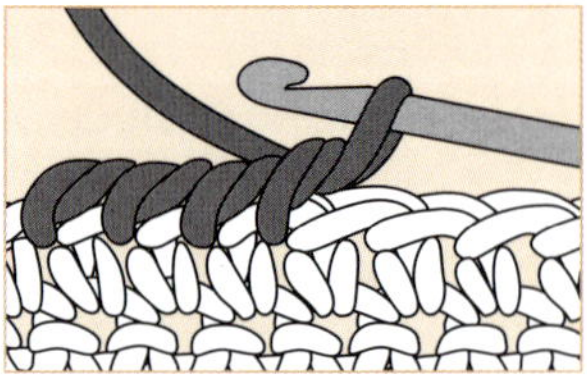

POM-POM

Cut a piece of cardboard 1" wide x 2" long (2.5 cm x 5 cm).

Holding one strand of each color, wind yarn around the cardboard until it is approximately ½" (12 mm) thick in the middle ***(Fig. E)***.

Carefully slip the yarn off the cardboard and firmly tie an 18" (45.5 cm) length of White around the middle ***(Fig. F)***. Leave yarn ends long enough to attach the pom-pom. Cut the loops on both ends and trim the pom-pom into a smooth ball ***(Fig. G)***.

Fig. E

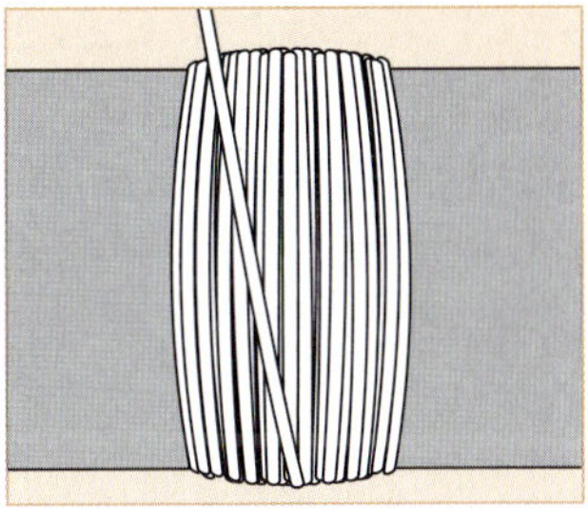

Fig. F

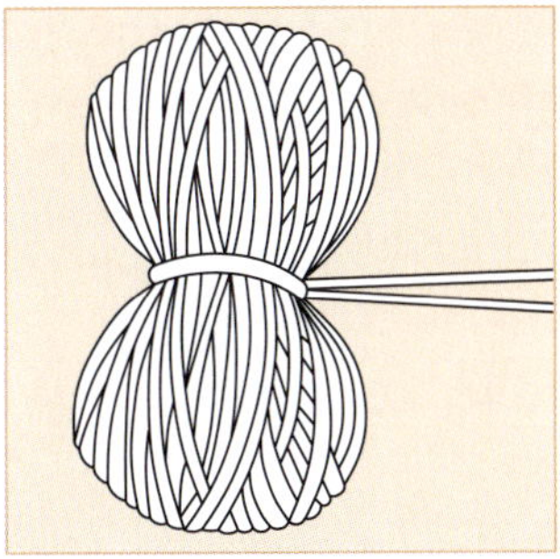

Fig. G

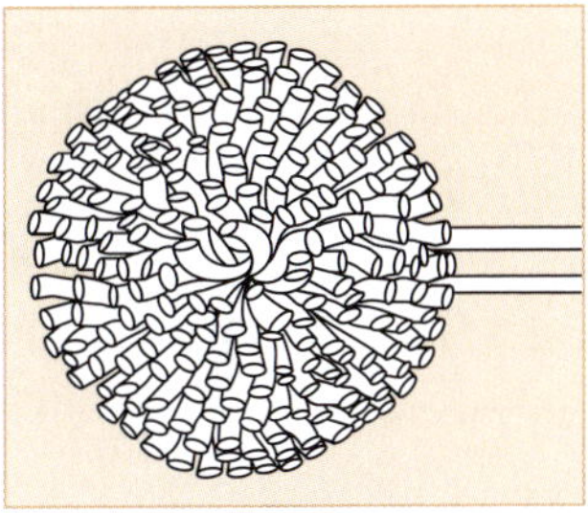

Attach pom-pom to top of Hat.

SNEAKER (Make 2)
SIZE INFORMATION

Small: 2" wide x 3" long
(5 cm x 7.5 cm)
Medium: 2" wide x 3½" long
(5 cm x 9 cm)

Size Note: We have printed the instructions for the sizes in different colors to make it easier for you to find:
- Size Small in Blue
- Size Medium in Pink

Instructions in Black apply to both sizes.

Use smaller size hook throughout.

SOLE (Make 2 for **each** sneaker)

With White, ch 8{10}.

Rnd 1 (Right side)**:** Sc in second ch from hook and in each ch across to last ch, 4 hdc in last ch; working in free loops of beginning ch ***(Fig. 1, page 45)***, sc in next 5{7} chs, 3 sc in next ch; join with slip st to first sc: 18{22} sts.

Note: Loop a short piece of yarn around any stitch to mark Rnd 1 as **right** side.

Rnd 2: Ch 1, sc in same st as joining and in next 3{5} sc, hdc in next 2 sc, 2 dc in each of next 4 hdc, hdc in next 2 sc, sc in next 3{5} sc, 2 sc in each of last 3 sc; join with slip st to first sc: 25{29} sts.

Rnd 3: Ch 2 (**does not count as a st, now and throughout**), hdc in same st as joining and in next 6{8} sts, 2 hdc in next dc, (hdc in next dc, 2 hdc in next dc) 3 times, hdc in next 5{7} sts, (sc in next sc, 2 sc in next sc) 3 times; join with slip st to first hdc, finish off: 32{36} sts.

On one Sole, place split ring marker or scrap yarn in Front Loop Only of fifth{seventh} hdc made on Rnd 3 for st placement ***(Fig. 2, page 45)***.

Joining: Hold two Soles with **wrong** sides together, matching sts, and marked Sole on bottom. Do **not** begin with slip knot on hook. Holding Orange to the back and working through **both** loops of **both** pieces, insert hook in any st on Rnd 3, YO and pull up a loop, slip st in each st around; cut yarn. Remove hook from loop. Insert hook from **back** to **front** through center of first st, hook loop and draw through, YO and pull end through loop.

SIDES

Row 1 (Right side)**:** With marked Sole away from you and working in Back Loops Only, join Grey with sc in marked loop ***(see Joining With Sc, page 45)***; remove marker, sc in next 15{19} sts, leave remaining 16 sts unworked: 16{20} sc.

Row 2: Ch 2, turn; dc in both loops of each sc across.

Row 3: Ch 1, turn; sc in each dc across.

Rows 4 thru 6{8}: Repeat Rows 2 and 3, 1{2} time(s); then repeat Row 2 once **more**.

Finish off.

Trim: With **right** side facing, join Orange with slip st in first dc on Sides; slip st in each dc across; finish off.

TOE

Row 1: With **right** side facing and working in Back Loops Only of Sole, join White with sc in first unworked st; sc in each sc across: 16 sc.

Row 2: Ch 1, turn; working in both loops, sc in first sc, hdc in next 3 sc, dc in next 8 sc, hdc in next 3 sc, sc in last sc.

Row 3: Turn; working in Back Loops Only and beginning in first sc, sc2tog twice, dc2tog 4 times, sc2tog twice: 8 sts.

Row 4: Ch 1, turn; working in both loops, sc in first 2 sc, dc in next 4 dc, sc in last 2 sc; finish off.

TONGUE

Row 1: With **right** side facing, join Grey with sc in first sc on Toe; sc in each st across.

Rows 2 thru 9{11}: Ch 1, turn; sc in each sc across.

Finish off.

With White, sew end of first 3 rows on Sides to end of rows on Toe.

LACES

With White, ch 80{85}; finish off.

Using photo as a guide for placement and beginning at the bottom of the Sides, weave Laces through end of rows.

SPORTY SNEAKERS & HAT

SHOPPING LIST

Yarn (Medium Weight)

[4 ounces, 203 yards (113 grams, 186 meters) per skein]:

- ☐ Grey - 1 skein
- ☐ White - 1 skein
- ☐ Peach - 1 skein

Crochet Hooks

- ☐ Size F (3.75 mm) **and**
- ☐ Size H (5 mm)

  or sizes needed for gauge

Additional Supplies

- ☐ Split ring marker or scrap yarn
- ☐ Yarn needle

GAUGE INFORMATION

Hat

Gauge Swatch: 3" (7.5 cm) square

With larger size hook and Grey, ch 11.

Row 1: Sc in second ch from hook and in each ch across: 10 sc.

Rows 2-12: Ch 1, turn; sc in each sc across.

Finish off.

Sneakers

Gauge Swatch: 2" wide x 3{3½}" long/5 cm x 7.5{9} cm

With smaller size hook, work same as Sole: 32{36} sts.

STITCH GUIDE

SINGLE CROCHET 2 TOGETHER ***(abbreviated sc2tog)***

Pull up a loop in each of next 2 sts, YO and draw through all 3 loops on hook **(counts as one sc)**.

DOUBLE CROCHET 2 TOGETHER ***(abbreviated dc2tog)*** (uses next 2 sts)

★ YO, insert hook in next st, YO and pull up a loop, YO and draw through 2 loops on hook; repeat from ★ once **more**, YO and draw through all 3 loops on hook **(counts as one dc)**.

HAT

Finished Size: 14" (35.5 cm) circumference

Use larger size hook throughout.

With Peach and leaving a long end for sewing, ch 46.

Rnd 1 (Right side)**:** Sc in second ch from hook and in each ch across; cut Peach, with Grey, join with slip st to first sc ***(Fig. 4, page 46)***: 45 sc.

Note: Loop a short piece of yarn around any stitch to mark Rnd 1 as **right** side.

Rnd 2: Ch 3 (**counts as first dc**), pull up a loop in same st and in each of next 2 sc, YO and draw through all 4 loops on hook, ch 1, ★ pull up a loop in same st and in each of next 2 sc, YO and draw through all 4 loops on hook, ch 1; repeat from ★ around; drop Grey, with White, join with slip st to first dc: 23 sts and 22 ch-1 sps.

Rnd 3: Ch 1, sc in same st as joining and in each st and each ch-1 sp around; drop White, with Grey, join with slip st to first sc: 45 sc.

Rnds 4-13: Repeat Rnds 2 and 3, 4 times; at end of Rnd 13; cut White: 45 sc.

Rnd 14: Ch 1, sc in same st as joining and in next 2 sc, sc2tog, (sc in next 3 sc, sc2tog) around; join with slip st to first sc: 36 sc.

Rnd 15: Ch 1, sc in same st as joining and in next sc, sc2tog, (sc in next 2 sc, sc2tog) around; join with slip st to first sc: 27 sc.

Rnd 16: Ch 1, sc in same st as joining, sc2tog, (sc in next sc, sc2tog) around; join with slip st to first sc: 18 sc.

Rnd 17: Ch 1, beginning in same st as joining, sc2tog around; join with slip st to first sc: 9 sc.

Rnd 18: Sc in each sc around; join with slip st to first sc, finish off leaving a long end for sewing.

Thread yarn needle with long end and weave needle through sts on Rnd 18 ***(Fig. 5, page 46)***, gather tightly and secure end.

Thread yarn needle with beginning end and sew through chs at base of first and last sc; secure end.

SNEAKER (Make 2)
SIZE INFORMATION

Small: 2" wide x 3" long (5 cm x 7.5 cm)

Medium: 2" wide x 3½" long (5 cm x 9 cm)

Size Note: We have printed the instructions for the sizes in different colors to make it easier for you to find:

- Size Small in Blue
- Size Medium in Pink

Instructions in Black apply to both sizes.

Use smaller size hook throughout.

SOLE (Make 2 for **each** sneaker)

With Grey, ch 8{10}.

Rnd 1 (Right side)**:** Sc in second ch from hook and in each ch across to last ch, 4 hdc in last ch; working in free loops of beginning ch ***(Fig. 1, page 45)***, sc in next 5{7} chs, 3 sc in next ch; join with slip st to first sc: 18{22} sts.

Note: Loop a short piece of yarn around any stitch to mark Rnd 1 as **right** side.

Rnd 2: Ch 1, sc in same st as joining and in next 3{5} sc, hdc in next 2 sc, 2 dc in each of next 4 hdc, hdc in next 2 sc, sc in next 3{5} sc, 2 sc in each of last 3 sc; join with slip st to first sc: 25{29} sts.

Rnd 3: Ch 2 (**does not count as a st**), hdc in same st as joining and in next 6{8} sts, 2 hdc in next dc, (hdc in next dc, 2 hdc in next dc) 3 times, hdc in next 5{7} sts, (sc in next sc, 2 sc in next sc) 3 times; join with slip st to first hdc, finish off: 32{36} sts.

On one Sole for each sneaker, place split ring marker or scrap yarn in Front Loop Only of third hdc made on Rnd 3 for st placement ***(Fig. 2, page 45)***.

Joining: Hold two Soles with **wrong** sides together, matching sts, and marked Sole on bottom. Do **not** begin with slip knot on hook. Holding White to the back and working through **both** loops of **both** pieces, insert hook in any st on Rnd 3, YO and pull up a loop, slip st in each st around; cut yarn. Remove hook from loop. Insert hook from **back** to **front** through center of first st, hook loop and draw through, YO and pull end through loop.

SIDES & TOE

Rnd 1 (Right side)**:** With marked Sole away from you and working in Back Loops Only, join White with sc in marked loop ***(see Joining With Sc, page 45)***; remove marker, sc in each st around; join with slip st to first sc: 32{36} sc.

Rnd 2: Ch 1, working in both loops, sc in same st as joining and in next 13{15} sc, hdc in next 4 sc, dc in next 8 sc, hdc in next 4 sc, sc in last 2{4} sc; join with slip st to first sc.

Rnd 3: Ch 1, sc in same st as joining, dc in next 10 sc, sc in next 3{5} sc, sc2tog twice, dc2tog 4 times, sc2tog twice, sc in last 2{4} sc; join with slip st to first sc: 24{28} sts.

Rnd 4: Ch 1, sc in same st as joining and in next 13{15} sts, dc2tog 4 times, sc in last 2{4} sc; join with slip st to first sc: 20{24} sts.

Rnd 5: Slip st in next 14{16} sc, sc in next dc, place marker in sc just made for Front Tab placement, sc in next 5 sts, slip st in last 0{2} sc ***(see Zeros, page 44)***; finish off.

FRONT TAB

With **right** side facing, join Grey with slip st in marked sc, remove marker; ch 2, dc in same st and in next 4 sts, (dc, ch 2, slip st) in next st, leave remaining sts unworked; finish off.

LACES

With Peach, ch 25; finish off.

Using photo as a guide for placement, insert chain from **back** to **front** on Rnd 4, then back down on opposite side. Bring chain up on Rnd 3, then back down on opposite side and secure on the inside.

GENERAL INSTRUCTIONS

ABBREVIATIONS

BPdc	Back Post double crochet(s)
ch(s)	chain(s)
cm	centimeters
dc	double crochet(s)
dc2tog	double crochet 2 together
FPdc	Front Post double crochet(s)
hdc	half double crochet(s)
mm	millimeters
Rnd(s)	Round(s)
sc	single crochet(s)
sc2tog	single crochet 2 together
sp(s)	space(s)
st(s)	stitch(es)
tr	treble crochet(s)
YO	yarn over

SYMBOLS & TERMS

★ — work instructions following ★ as many **more** times as indicated in addition to the first time.

( ) or **[ ]** — work enclosed instructions **as many** times as specified by the number immediately following **or** work all enclosed instructions in the stitch or space indicated **or** contains explanatory remarks.

colon (:) — the number(s) given after a colon at the end of a row or round denote(s) the number of stitches or spaces you should have on that row or round.

CROCHET TERMINOLOGY		
UNITED STATES		INTERNATIONAL
slip stitch (slip st)	=	single crochet (sc)
single crochet (sc)	=	double crochet (dc)
half double crochet (hdc)	=	half treble crochet (htr)
double crochet (dc)	=	treble crochet (tr)
treble crochet (tr)	=	double treble crochet (dtr)
double treble crochet (dtr)	=	triple treble crochet (ttr)
triple treble crochet (tr tr)	=	quadruple treble crochet (qtr)
skip	=	miss

BEGINNER	Projects for first-time crocheters using basic stitches. Minimal shaping.
EASY	Projects using yarn with basic stitches, repetitive stitch patterns, simple color changes, and simple shaping and finishing.
INTERMEDIATE	Projects using a variety of techniques, such as basic lace patterns or color patterns, mid-level shaping and finishing.
EXPERIENCED	Projects with intricate stitch patterns, techniques and dimension, such as non-repeating patterns, multi-color techniques, fine threads, small hooks, detailed shaping and refined finishing.

GAUGE

Exact gauge is **essential** for proper fit. Before beginning your project, make the sample swatch in the yarn and hook specified. After completing the swatch, measure it, counting your stitches and rows or rounds carefully. If your piece is larger or smaller than specified, **make another, changing hook size to get the correct gauge**. Keep trying until you find the size hook that will give you the specified gauge.

MARKERS

Markers are used to help distinguish the beginning of each round being worked. Place a 2" (5 cm) scrap piece of yarn before the first stitch of each round, moving the marker after each round is complete.

When marking a stitch, use a split ring marker or a scrap piece of yarn.

ZEROS

To consolidate the length of a pattern, zeros are sometimes used so that both sizes can be combined. For example, slip st in last 0{2} sc means the first size would do nothing and the second size would slip st in last 2 sc.

Yarn Weight Symbol & Names	LACE 0	SUPER FINE 1	FINE 2	LIGHT 3	MEDIUM 4	BULKY 5	SUPER BULKY 6	JUMBO 7
Type of Yarns in Category	Fingering, size 10 crochet thread	Sock, Fingering, Baby	Sport, Baby	DK, Light Worsted	Worsted, Afghan, Aran	Chunky, Craft, Rug	Super Bulky, Roving	Jumbo, Roving
Crochet Gauge* Ranges in Single Crochet to 4" (10 cm)	32-42 sts**	21-32 sts	16-20 sts	12-17 sts	11-14 sts	8-11 sts	6-9 sts	5 sts and fewer
Advised Hook Size Range	Steel*** 6 to 8, Regular hook B-1	B-1 to E-4	E-4 to 7	7 to I-9	I-9 to K-10½	K-10½ to M/N-13	M/N-13 to Q	Q and larger

*GUIDELINES ONLY: The chart above reflects the most commonly used gauges and hook sizes for specific yarn categories.

** Lace weight yarns are usually crocheted with larger hooks to create lacy openwork patterns. Accordingly, a gauge range is difficult to determine. Always follow the gauge stated in your pattern.

*** Steel crochet hooks are sized differently from regular hooks–the higher the number, the smaller the hook, which is the reverse of regular hook sizing.

CROCHET HOOKS	
U.S.	Metric mm
B-1	2.25
C-2	2.75
D-3	3.25
E-4	3.5
F-5	3.75
G-6	4
7	4.5
H-8	5
I-9	5.5
J-10	6
K-10½	6.5
L-11	8
M/N-13	9
N/P-15	10
P/Q	15
Q	16
S	19

JOINING WITH SC

When instructed to join with sc, begin with a slip knot on hook. Insert hook in stitch indicated, YO and pull up a loop, YO and draw through both loops on hook.

JOINING WITH DC

When instructed to join with dc, begin with a slip knot on hook. YO, holding loop on hook, insert hook in stitch indicated, YO and pull up a loop (3 loops on hook), (YO and draw through 2 loops on hook) twice.

FREE LOOPS OF A CHAIN

When instructed to work in free loops of a chain, work in loop indicated by arrow ***(Fig. 1)***.

Fig. 1

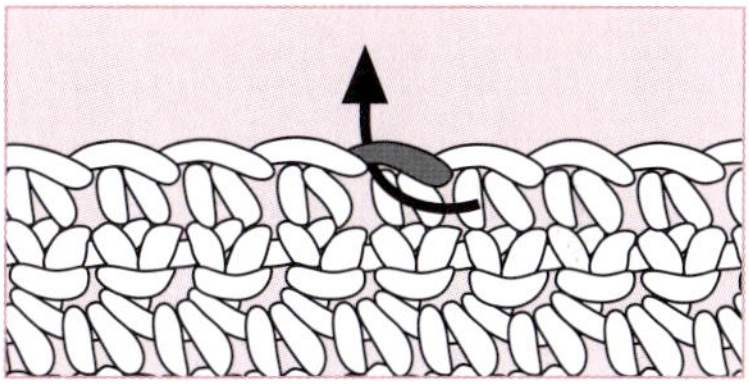

BACK OR FRONT LOOPS ONLY

Work only in loop(s) indicated by arrow ***(Fig. 2)***.

Fig. 2

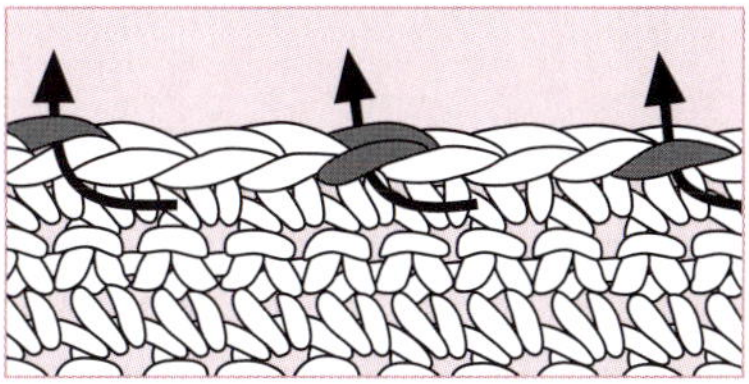

WORKING IN FRONT OF OR BEHIND A STITCH

Work in stitch indicated, inserting hook in direction of arrow ***(Figs. 3a & b)***.

Fig. 3a

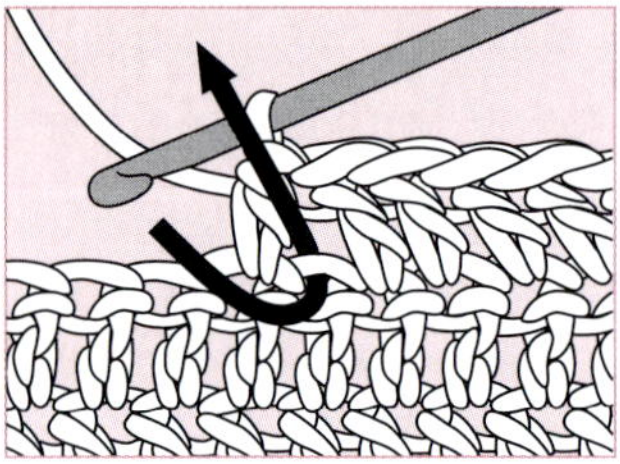

Fig. 3b

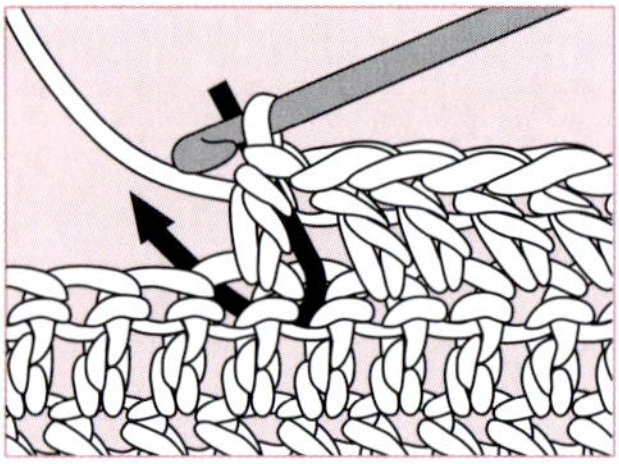

CHANGING COLORS

Drop yarn, insert hook in first stitch, with new yarn, YO and draw through stitch and loop on hook ***(Fig. 4)***.

Fig. 4

WEAVING THRU STITCHES

Weave yarn end through the stitches ***(Fig. 5)*** and gather to close.

Fig. 5

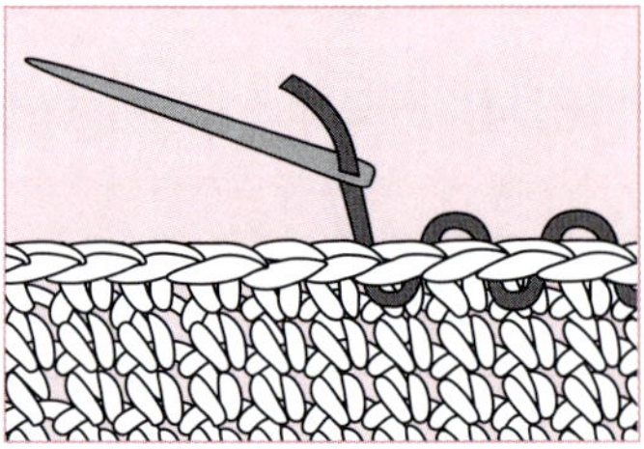

Meet Kristi Simpson

Kristi Simpson enjoys designing cute baby gifts that mothers will love using. “There’s just something special about having a handmade gift,” she says. “It’s personal and unique.”

Inspired by her love of yarn, she creates crochet and knit patterns with a fresh and modern touch. The mother of five became hooked on crochet after teaching herself so she could help her daughter make a scarf from a “learn to crochet” kit that was a gift.

“I loved it from the beginning,” she says. “I was amazed that I could take a string of yarn and create something so useful and pretty! Needless to say, I never stopped!”

Other Leisure Arts books featuring Kristi’s designs include *Urban Slouch Hats* (#6796), *Easy Essential Bags* (#6795), *Animal Baby Bibs* (#6850), *Sweet & Sporty Diaper Covers* (#6719), and more to come soon. Visit kristisimpson.net or find her on Ravelry, Facebook, and Pinterest.

Yarn Information

The items in this book were made using medium weight yarn. Any brand of medium weight yarn may be used. Remember, to arrive at the finished size, it is the GAUGE/TENSION that is important, not the brand of yarn.

For your convenience, listed below are the yarns used to create our photography models. Because yarn manufacturers make frequent changes in their product lines, you may sometimes find it necessary to use a substitute yarn or to search for the discontinued product at alternate suppliers (locally or online).

CASUAL BOOTS & HAT
Premier® Yarns Deborah Norville™ Collection Everyday® Soft Worsted
Taupe - #100-52 Chinchilla
Green - #100-30 Glass

CASUAL LOAFERS & HAT
Lion Brand® Vanna's Choice®
Tan - #099 Linen
Blue - #108 Dusty Blue

HIGH-TOP MOCCASINS & HAT
Premier® Yarns Deborah Norville™ Collection Everyday® Soft Worsted
Grey - #100-23 Mist
Green - #100-16 Kiwi
Blue - #100-17 Azure
Gold - #100-28 Mustard

LACY CUFF BOOTS & HAT
Lion Brand® Vanna's Choice®
Grey - #149 Silver Grey
Rose - #112 Raspberry
White - #100 White

HIGH-TOP SNEAKERS & HAT
Red Heart® Soft®
White - #4600 White
Grey - #9440 Light Grey Heather
Orange - #4422 Tangerine

SPORTY SNEAKERS & HAT
Premier® Yarns Deborah Norville™ Collection Everyday® Soft Worsted
Grey - #100-23 Mist
White - #100-01 Snow White
Peach - #100-54 Coral

Production Team: Instructional/Technical Editor - Lois J. Long; Editorial Writer - Susan Frantz Wiles; Graphic Artist - Kellie McAnulty; Senior Graphic Artist - Lora Puls; Photo Stylist - Lori Wenger; and Photographer - Jason Masters.

Booties made and instructions tested by Kellie Duncan and Barbara Schou.